Lightning Bolt Books™

Dangerous Volcanoes

Lola Schaefer

Lerner Publications ◆ Minneapolis

Lerner Publications Company
An imprint of Lerner Publishing Group, Inc.
241 First Avenue North
Minneapolis, MN 55401 USA

For reading levels and more information, look up this title at www.lernerbooks.com.

Main body text set in Billy Infant Regular. Typeface provided by SparkType.

Photo Editor: Cynthia Zemlicka

Library of Congress Cataloging-in-Publication Data

Names: Schaefer, Lola M., 1950- author.
Title: Dangerous volcanoes / Lola Schaefer.
Description: Minneapolis : Lerner Publications, [2022] | Series: Lightning bolt books - earth in danger | Includes bibliographical references and index. | Audience: Ages 6–9 | Audience: Grades 2–3 | Summary: "Volcano eruptions can be devastating. Learn how volcanoes are formed, what happens when they erupt, and how to stay safe from eruptions. A back matter feature highlights the story of someone who survived a volcano"— Provided by publisher.
Identifiers: LCCN 2021010516 (print) | LCCN 2021010517 (ebook) | ISBN 9781728441443 (library binding) | ISBN 9781728444864 (ebook)
Subjects: LCSH: Volcanoes—Juvenile literature.
Classification: LCC QE522 .S2947 2022 (print) | LCC QE522 (ebook) | DDC 551.21—dc23

LC record available at https://lccn.loc.gov/2021010516
LC ebook record available at https://lccn.loc.gov/2021010517

Manufactured in the United States of America
1-49915-49758-5/20/2021

Table of Contents

Volcanoes Erupt

Gas, steam, and ash burst into the air. They rise higher and higher in a tall cloud.

Red-hot lava spews out and flows downhill. It burns everything in its path. This is a volcanic eruption.

Gas vents near the Puu Oo crater in Hawaii.

A volcano is a vent in Earth's crust. Hot gases, rocks, and lava can escape through the vent.

Active volcanoes have erupted in the past and might erupt again. The United States has more than 150 active volcanoes.

Mount Katmai in Alaska is one of the state's 141 volcanoes.

How Do Volcanoes Work?

Earth's core is very hot. The temperature ranges from 7,952°F (4,400°C) to 10,800°F (6,000°C), as hot as the sun.

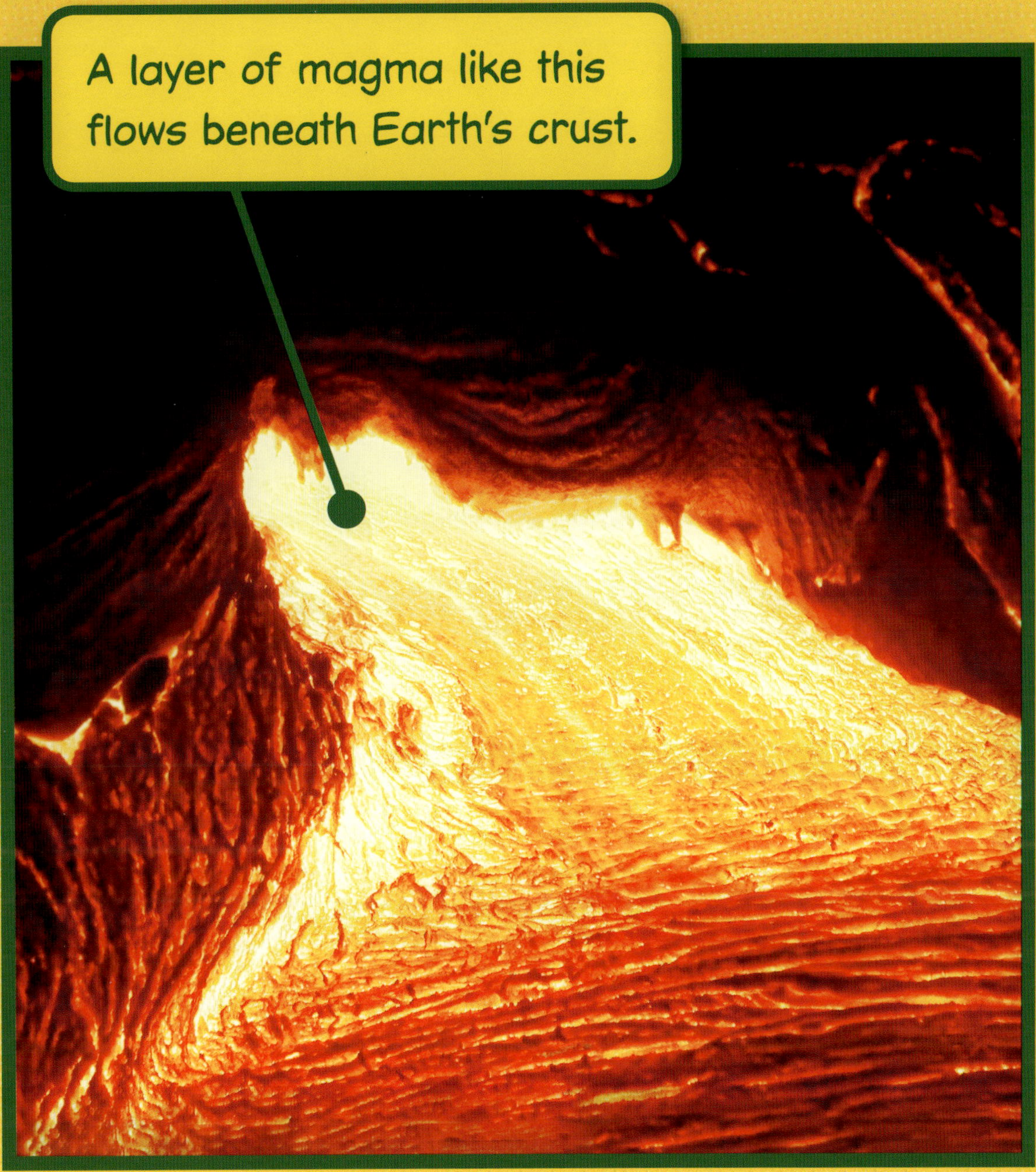

The heat in Earth's core melts rock beneath its crust. This molten rock is called magma.

Earth's crust is made of plates of rock. These are called tectonic plates. As they move, steam and molten rock escape through vents in volcanoes.

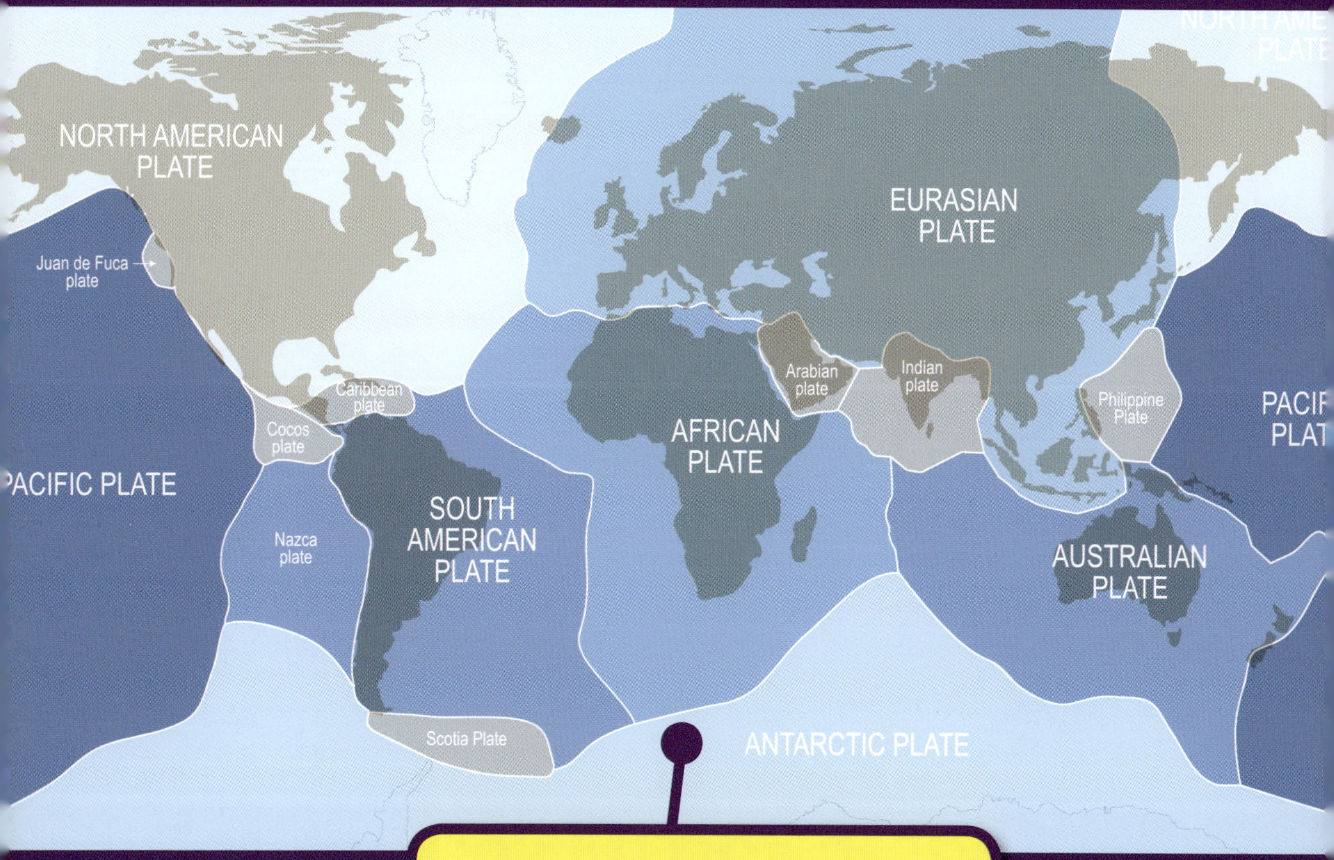

This map shows Earth's tectonic plates.

Climate change can affect volcanoes. It makes eruptions bigger and more frequent.

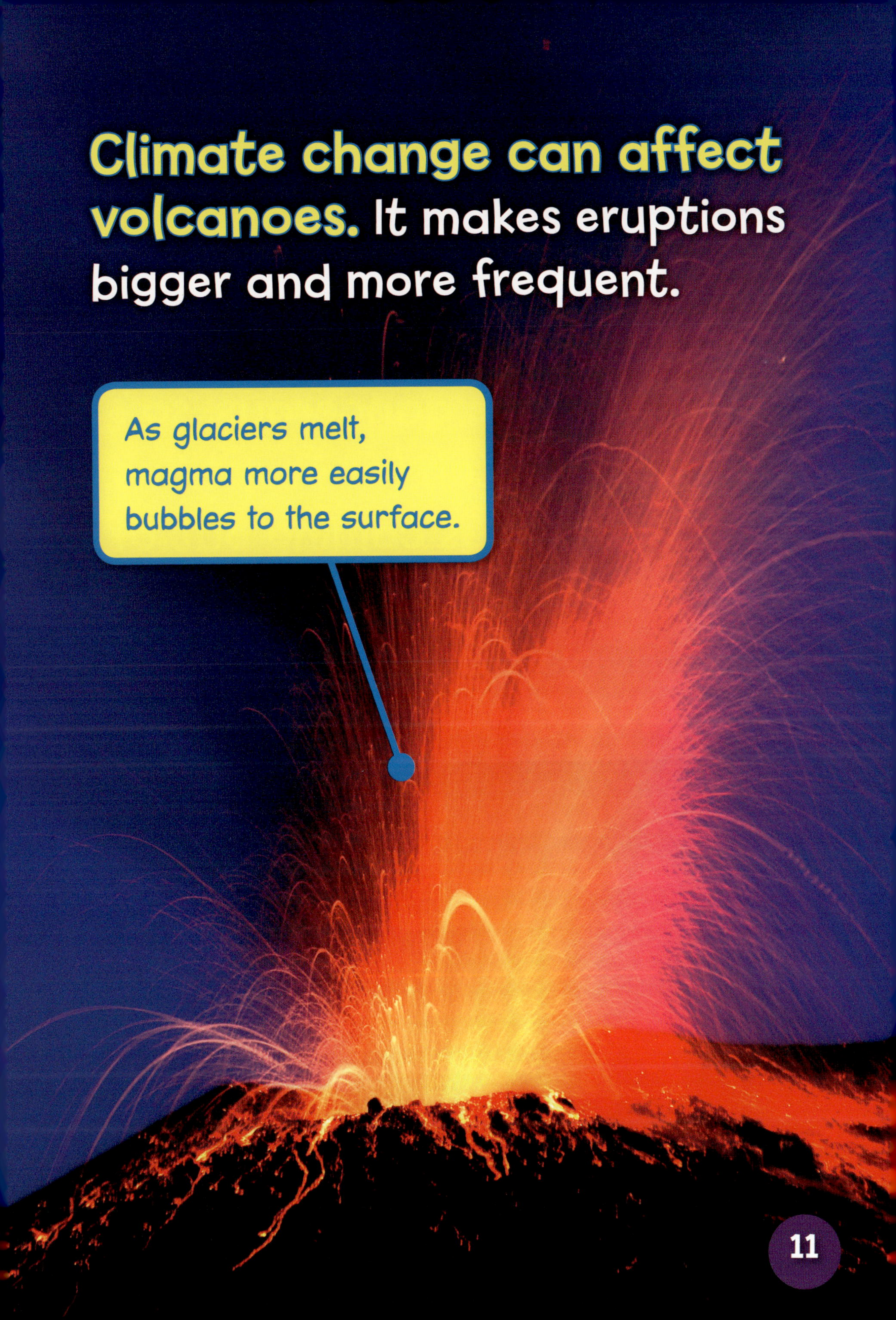

As glaciers melt, magma more easily bubbles to the surface.

Dangerous Volcanoes

Volcanoes are dangerous, so scientists watch for eruptions. Steam or gases coming out of the top is one warning sign. Earthquakes are another.

Sometimes volcanoes surprise scientists. If scientists think an eruption will happen, they warn people to stay away.

A scientist looks at a graph of an earthquake that struck Christchurch, New Zealand, in 2011.

This house was buried by volcanic lava and ash.

Explosive eruptions can destroy life in a large area. Effusive eruptions are milder but can last much longer.

Ash and gas can stay in the air for a long time and block sunlight, cooling Earth.

Eruptions can have big effects. Clouds of gas and ash rise into the air and travel. They can cool Earth for more than a year.

Staying Safe

If you live near an active volcano, be ready with an escape plan. Watch the news for warnings. If you are asked to leave, do so quickly.

During an eruption, stay miles away from the volcano. Do not try to get closer.

Volcanic ash can travel thousands of miles.

Gases and ash can hurt your throat and lungs.

Remain indoors. If you are outside, the gases and ash could burn your eyes. You might cough, or your skin might sting.

Volcanoes are dangerous. But their ash feeds the soil. Their lava makes new landforms. Volcanoes are an important part of nature!

After Mount St. Helens in Washington State erupted in 1980, the valley around it grew back lush and green.

I Survived a Volcano

Richard Ford worked on Mount St. Helens as a forester. For months, he saw the volcano vent releasing steam and ash high into the air. Scientists blocked off the possible blast site to keep workers and visitors safe from danger. On May 18, 1980, Mount St. Helens erupted. Ford was at home and not on the mountain. Since he was far away, he survived.

Volcano Facts

- In the past two hundred years, more than fifty volcanoes in the US have erupted.
- When Mount St. Helens erupted, ash fell over 22,000 square miles (56,980 sq. km). It reached cities 370 miles (595 km) away.
- Some lavas can reach a temperature of 2,140°F (1,171°C), four times hotter than a kitchen oven.
- Yellowstone National Park has a supervolcano, an unusually large volcano. When it last erupted more than 640,000 years ago, it made a giant crater called a caldera.

Glossary

climate change: long-term changes in global temperature due to human activity

core: the center of Earth

crust: the hard, rocky covering of Earth

effusive: a type of volcanic eruption where lava pours out slowly

eruption: when a volcano throws out hot rock, ashes, gas, and lava with great force

lava: hot liquid rock that pours from a volcano during an eruption

magma: melted rock found beneath Earth's surface

vent: the shaft of a volcano through which steam, ash, and lava escape

Learn More

Daugey, Fleur. *Pop-Up Volcano!* New York: Thames and Hudson, 2020.

Kim, Carol. *Dangerous Earthquakes.* Minneapolis: Lerner Publications, 2022.

National Geographic Kids: Volcano
https://kids.nationalgeographic.com/science/article/volcano

Tarpley, Todd. *Oh, the Lavas That Flow! All about Volcanoes.* New York: Random House, 2021.

Time for Kids: What Are Volcanoes?
https://www.timeforkids.com/g34/volcanoes-2/

Weather Wiz Kids: Volcanoes
https://www.weatherwizkids.com/weather-volcano.htm

Index

Photo Acknowledgments

Image credits: Alaska Volcano Observatory/USGS, p. 4; Tomarchio Francesco/Shutterstock.com, p. 5; Felix Nendzig/Shutterstock.com, p. 6; National Park Service, p. 7; Johan Swanepoel/Shutterstock.com, p. 8; Ralf Lehmann/Shutterstock.com, p. 9; ttsz/Getty Images, p. 10; AZ68/Getty Images, p. 11; mlharing/Getty Images, p. 12; TED ALJIBE/AFP/Getty Images, p. 13; Mikael Damkier/Shutterstock.com, p. 14; andersen_oystein/Getty Images, p. 15; Ulet Ifansasti/Getty Images, p. 16; Andrea Savoca/EyeEm/Getty Images, p. 17; Dene' Miles/Shutterstock.com, p. 19; CGN089/Shutterstock.com, p. 18.

Cover image: Fernando Privitera/500px/Getty Images.